MAK

ARCHITECTURE
AS
ENACTMENT

SAM JACOB

CONTENTS

The danger is that it's just talk. Then again, the danger is that it's not. I believe you can speak things into existence.
Jay-Z, *Decoded*, 2010

REAL
FICTIONS

'The Great Roe', Woody Allen tells us, 'is a mythological beast with the head of a lion and the body of a lion, though not the same lion.' In the Great Roe, the fictional and the real combine into a seamless composite. Though radically spliced, the line between myth and biology is invisible — there's no way to tell where one begins and the other ends, which part is myth and which is real. Do its front paws walk on real ground and its rear on mythic landscapes? Or are both front and hindquarters real, with the myth being located in the splice? Other mythological creatures — the half-human, half-animal satyrs, fauns, centaurs and the like — distort reality into crypto-biological arrangements of pure fiction. The Great Roe, though, embodies a strange and absurd condition where the opposite conditions of fiction and reality are contained within the same physical entity. One does not undo the other. Instead, its idea (its mythic fiction) and its form (a real lion) coincide exactly.

In constructing this comedic absurdity, Allen has accidently provided us with a fitting description of the way architecture occupies the world. Because architecture, like the Great Roe, is simultaneously mythical and real. Mythical, in the sense that it is the invention of the society that creates it — the 'will of an epoch made into space', as Mies put it. Real, in the sense that it is the landscape that we inhabit. The perfect registration between these two states provides architecture with its own supernatural power: its prosaic appearance cloaks its mythic, imaginative origins entirely. To begin to understand architecture's Great Roe-ish state we must first think of how architecture mythologises and fictionalises itself, and then examine how it transmutes these fictions into reality.

Like a mythical beast, architecture emerges from the psycho-cultural landscape of its social, political and economic circumstances. Its body may be an exquisite corpse of (biologically impossible) architectural limbs, torsos, heads and tails, yet it is animated, active and alive—like Frankenstein's monster. At any given moment it projects its historical situation—the great teeming mass of narratives that prefigured its existence — into the contemporary world. And in doing so it fundamentally rewrites that history, splicing and sewing the narratives together to make a radical new proposition for the future.

The representation of history is, of course, highly politicised. As Churchill tells us, history is written by the victors. He suggests that history is at least part fiction, and that its writing is a spoil of war. In its own way, architecture is also a spoil of war, arising out of ideological, aesthetic, economic as well as military conflicts. But in contrast to written history, architecture's victorious narrative manifests itself as reality. It not only represents and illustrates this fictional history but physically embodies it, playing it out through substance, space and programme.

If we trace architecture's history, we can see that this radical re-enactment is a fundamental mode of its development. We might begin a historical survey of architecture's re-enactments with the Egyptian column, which was carved from stone to represent a tree trunk or a bundle of reeds. Right here, in a foundational moment, we see re-enactment as the primary architectural idea. The primitive tree-column returns just as it is being technologically superseded. The original gesture of the tree-column is radically altered through its re-enactment in stone, through its revival as a kind of ritualised symbol that celebrates its own origins.

In Greek architecture too we can read architecture's compulsion to re-enact. Not only is the Egyptian column re-staged in the Doric, Ionic and Corinthian orders, but re-enactment generates the entire language of classical architecture through the re-staging of primitive timber Greek temples. As with the Egyptian column, stone replaces timber, but here the entire structure is transubstantiated. And in this transformation, architecture represents its own origin just as it becomes something else. We see this in details such as triglyphs, the vertically channelled blocks in a Doric frieze that are understood as stone representations of the original timber end-beams—even though these beams are unnecessary in stone construction. Under them are stone *guttae* that re-enact the wooden pegs that would have been needed to stabilise a timber post-and-beam structure, but here they are rhetorical. In these examples, we see one construction technology re-enacted in another, creating paradoxes where the image of one intersects with the other's substance. These technological glitches are moments where the status of the re-enactment is made visible—like seeing a Civil War re-enactor on a mobile phone. They act like the splurges of a Warhol silkscreen or the howl of feedback, where the medium itself distorts the subject, where the act of reproduction becomes an active part of re-performance.

Through the unfolding of architectural history we see culturally, technologically or programmatically redundant fragments of architecture re-enacted. In each case, this re-enactment of a pre-existing image is a radical new iteration. Like Churchill's idea of history, architecture's re-enactment presents a partial and fictionalised narrative. What architecture chooses to re-enact, as well as the manner of its re-enactment, constitutes an ideological statement.

Fast-forwarding through history, we see Greek architectural language stretched around new Roman typologies. We see architecture's classical language resurrected (and re-invented) to ennoble and legitimise Renaissance culture. We see medieval forms of construction re-enacted by the arts and crafts movement as a means of opposition to the industrial revolution—a visual, material and structural analogue to its proto-socialist politics. And we see modernism's appropriation of the language of industrial buildings, where the grain stores of Buffalo, for example, are cited by Le Corbusier as 'the magnificent first fruits of the new age'. Modernism's re-performing of industrial architecture's logics of mechanisation and efficiency operated as a polemic. First it was a way of undermining the social and political hierarchies that Beaux-Arts architecture represented. Secondly it allowed modernism to lay claim to a pre-existing machine aesthetic, to propose an architecture already embedded in the contemporary condition it described.

In its freewheeling rewriting of the past, architecture uses history as a slingshot into the future. It endlessly re-stages itself, self-consciously folding its own past into its future, rewriting its own myth into its very fabric. At the same time it legitimises its new propositions by embedding them within lineages of existing languages, materials and typologies. The re-enactment's repetition of the existing helps to naturalise the shock of the new, declaring itself an inevitable product of historical circumstance. Architecture, then, mythologises its own creation while making a historical argument for itself and proposing a future world—all within the substance of its own body.

Architecture's preoccupation with re-staging itself is more than a disciplinary in-joke. And unlike, say, a civil war re-enactment, it never packs up and goes home because it *is* home (or anywhere else we might be). Rather, architecture's re-enactments are deadly serious and entirely real.

We could see architecture's re-enactment of history in the present as a kind of anachronic radicalism. Here, fragments of history are sucked out of their chronological order, emptied of their historical context, to make them available as devices, strategies, images and forms that can be piped full of other narratives and re-tasked to perform with alternative intent. These re-formed references, at once familiar and made strange, can then be deployed to validate and manifest a version of the present. Through re-enactment, architecture re-writes itself, making fictions a part of the real landscape that surrounds us.

Architecture's strategies of re-enactment remind us of what, in science fiction at least, is a peril of time travel: when you enter the past, you risk radically altering the future. Trample on a single prehistoric butterfly and you could return to an entirely different world. Architecture too possesses this ability to rewrite the present. Using powers of cultural fiction rather than imaginary technology, architecture mobilises the same potential as science fiction: the possibility of manufacturing multiple versions of the future out of the past.

AUTHENTIC
REPLICAS

AUTHENTIC REPLICAS

In Dearborn, Michigan, amongst the vast tracts of land owned by the Ford Corporation, stands Greenfield Village. It neighbours Ford's test-track, innovation and research buildings and the Ford River Rouge Complex which was, when completed in 1928, the largest integrated industrial plant in the world, with its six factories, docks dredged into the river, hundred miles of railroad track, power station and ore-processing plant. In the midst of this vast landscape of industrial production are two cultural centres also established by Henry Ford: a museum and a 'village'. The eponymous Henry Ford Museum incorporates into its architectural fabric a replica of Philadelphia's Independence Hall, a suggestive signal of what lies in store as we enter this autobiographical autoland where Henry Ford's self-image, Ford's corporate entity and American mythology merge into a military-industrial complex manufacturing cars and ideology in equal measure. This autographic landscape finds its conclusion in Greenfield Village.

To construct Greenfield Village, Ford purchased a series of historic buildings and moved them to the site. Using these dislocated fragments, he developed a technique that might be described as urban bricolage, arranging eighty-three 'authentic, historic structures' to form the image of an archetypal village with a Main Street, a central square, residential areas and so on.

Greenfield is an extreme example of the architectural re-enactment. We can use it here as a device to explore the generic architectural phenomenon of making the imaginary real. Though made out of 'real' things—real buildings relocated brick by brick from their original sites to a field in Dearborn—Greenfield is the manifestation of Ford's imagination. All of its authenticity serves to support this imaginary condition, to make it real.

Greenfield Village embodies Ford's educational philosophy of 'learning by doing', as opposed to academic knowledge (the target of his often quoted phrase, 'history is bunk'). Ford constructed the village as a means of educating students through direct experience. Greenfield, then, is a mechanism to deliver history as a set of experiences that make tangible Ford's vision of America as a nation founded on enterprise. Greenfield's synthetic authenticity reads both as a place and as a fiction through which Henry Ford could write his own version of history.

Entering Greenfield we pass a station, cross the tracks on which an authentic steam train endlessly circles the village, go by a working farm, some paddocks with horses, and turn onto Main Street. Here we find the Wright Brothers' bicycle shop. Their workshop is in the back, with a half-built flying machine and tools laid out as though Orville and Wilbur had just stepped outside for a moment.

Opposite is the Heinz house, complete with the basement in which an eight-year-old Henry John Heinz began bottling horseradish sauce. Both now neighbour each other, symbols of American modernity—of flight and ketchup—rearranged into small-town scale. Though the buildings are real, they manufacture a fiction though Ford's collapsing of space and time.

Further on, a stone cottage and a forge relocated from the English Cotswolds sit on a hill above a farmhouse from Connecticut and a windmill from Cape Cod. The forge is active and produces things used to repair the village, so that in Dearborn even maintenance becomes a kind of embedded performance producing authentic-replicas that are gradually replacing the real-authentic building components piece by piece.

Nearby is Noah Webster's home, where the first American dictionary was written, and a house originally built by slaves on the Hermitage Plantation in Savannah, Georgia. We see the Logan County courthouse where Abraham Lincoln practised law. And, of course, Henry Ford's childhood home, moved here from its original site three miles away.

The village operates as a scenographic backdrop against which epochal events such as the Civil War are re-enacted and costumed interpreters perform period tasks like farming, sewing and cooking. You might meet a jobbing actor performing the role of Edison holding a press conference within his laboratory, casting us as members of the press and overeagerly re-enacting a personality within a real-life, once-removed, authentic-fake environment.

Re-enactment is Greenfield's core mode. It opened on the fiftieth anniversary of Edison's invention of the electric light bulb, and the opening ceremony saw (the real) Edison re-enact this moment in his rebuilt and relocated laboratories. Ford asked Edison to sit on the upper floor of the main workshop. Ford himself was downstairs, waiting for Edison to perform—to shout out with Eurekean glee as he might have done fifty years before. On hearing the cry, Ford rushed upstairs, demanding that the chair Edison had been sitting on be nailed to the floor, to forever fix this re-staged moment.

Driving dizzying circuits of Greenfield's roads are a series of Model T Fords. These are replicas, built to commemorate the centenary of their first production. One pulls up—like a carriage in a theme park ride—and offers a personalised tour of the village. Our driver, Randy, tells us the story of the replica Model Ts. Like all cars—for these fakes are real cars—they break down, even crash into each other. Over time, Randy suggests, all of the parts of all of the cars have been swapped around, replaced or otherwise renewed. These replicas, then, are not even themselves anymore. And in this they rehearse the classical paradox of the ship of Theseus. Plutarch, writing in 75 AD, describes this philosophical problem. As a memorial, the Greek hero's ship had been preserved in an ocean-ready state by the citizens of Athens. Over time, however, it began to rot and its planks were replaced one by one until none of the originals remained. Yet the ship was still there. This, Plutarch suggests, presents a paradox: is the ship still Theseus's? Or is it entirely new? Does an object or entity remain the same if it is replaced wholesale, piece by piece? Or what happens if the replaced parts are used to build a second version of the object?

This question of identifying the authentic — of trying to point to the real — is key to the idea of the re-enactment. The re-enactment maintains the image of the real. It maintains the Model T as a real object. But it also makes it unreal — a representation of itself. These, then, are real, unreal, authentic replicas tootling around Greenfield. If the object itself is freighted with rival forms of authenticity — actual and representational — both serve to re-enact an idea of the real. Greenfield Village is a carefully curated ideology dressed up in layers of legitimising authenticity. Its architecture literally reconstructs and performs history as a way of naturalising Ford's narrative of American modernity.

Before leaving Greenfield Village we could make one last stop at Edison's resurrected laboratory, where we find an object that can be read as a parable of the reproduction and its ability to manufacture reality. There, on a table, is a display of Edison's electric pen. The pen has an electric motor that drives a needle that perforates a sheet of paper that in turn acts as a stencil, allowing multiple copies of the document to be printed in a press. Initially successful, the device was soon superseded by other forms of copying technology. Edison's electric pen, however, found another use, when it was modified by Samuel O'Reilly in 1891 to become the first electric tattoo needle. In repurposing Edison's technology, O'Reilly transformed a device intended to produce copies into a way of indelibly marking our own bodies. Instead of producing replicas, the copy machine now etches fictions into the very dermis of the real.

Of course, Greenfield Village is not a village but an island whose idealised fantasy is only made possible by its separation from the world at large. Its edge—like the white-line edge of a sports field—delineates the space within which a particular set of rules and forms of behaviour operate, a rule-set that cannot exist beyond those boundaries. It is a weak form of reality, despite all of its authenticity, its three-dimensional spatiality and its scale. It reflects a theatrical rather than an architectural condition of reality, one where we have to suspend our disbelief to participate—where we are totally immersed in its physicality, but remain separate from it: spectators rather than actors.

Like raising a vein, the re-enactment exposes architecture's own mechanics of performance and enactment, so that we can see more clearly its methods of manufacturing the imaginary within the real. In the re-enactment, where the fictional and the real are marshalled and negotiated into experience, architecture's ability to make real is expressed in bolder form. The re-enactment, then, despite its often exceptional, out-of-ordinary status, serves us here as a more entrenched, deeper grooved version of architecture's general condition.

ENACTING
ARCHITECTURE

We can think of the world, or rather of the world as we have made it, as a composite of both myth and reality. The mythological comprises the ideas and ideologies, the meanings and beliefs that make up our cultural narrative. These are the things we write, draw, say and think. This world is imagined and described through media such as art, literature and philosophy. So, for example, a novel gives us a description of the world that helps us to understand our relationship to the world or to each other. But it does not directly alter the substance of the world. Its force bears solely on our imagination and perception.

The real, on the other hand, is the stuff we can touch, weigh, measure in an empirical manner—the physical facts of our environment. This world might be made using mediums such as science, design and law—things that attempt to manifest the real as indisputable, tangible fact.

These worlds of myth and reality, though existing in close proximity and formed in direct relation to each other, remain distinct from one another. And mostly these distinctions between fact and fiction, between imaginary and real, between stage and street, are clear. There are few things that operate like the Great Roe, that straddle both worlds and exist as both fiction and reality simultaneously. This, however, is architecture's special condition.

MAKE IT REAL

It falls to architecture to make the imaginary real. Architecture, real in its physical presence, is at the same time also an imaginary thing. Even the most prosaic piece of the built environment originates first with an idea that might be drawn from the broad spectrum of motivations to build: commercial, symbolic, cultural, social, egotistical, love, sadness and so on. The actualisation of the imaginary into the real is architecture's fundamental mode, its inescapable condition as a medium. Architecture, we can say, in a manner unique to its discipline, transforms the fictional, the imagined and the ideological into the flesh-and-blood physicality that engulfs us. It takes an idea or ideology and manifests this in built form — not as illustration, not as representation, not as a description, but *actually*.

For example, a building like Frank Lloyd Wright's Johnson Wax Headquarters, with its open, clerestory-lit Great Workroom, demonstrates how the corporation is only made possible by its architecture. Thus the Great Workroom, where desk after clerical desk typed out corporate correspondence, is the manifestation of a particular idea of the corporation as a bureaucratic entity. It makes the idea of the organisation real by spatialising and materialising it. Architecture's built form, then, is simultaneously both the idea and the reality.

By beginning with the imaginary, and transforming this into an everyday reality, architecture reverses the polarity of fiction and reality associated with other forms of creative practice. Novels, movies and plays, for example, fictionalise the real. They use representations of the world as the site for manifesting the imaginary, relying on armatures and apparatuses such as page, screen or stage to create the conditions in which their fictional versions of reality can play out. From our vantage point as spectators we see these spaces as separated from the 'real' world, and have to suspend our disbelief in order to accept their claims to true description. Whatever their content, from the comic to the tragic, and however radical, they remain unreal. The same content performed outside of the narrative frame— on the street rather than the stage—would produce entirely different effects.

All art is, in this sense, abstract—an idea of reality hosted within a distinct frame. But architecture operates in the realm of the real, in an unmediated manner. We don't have to suspend our disbelief in order for its fiction to be real. It is there, pure fact, all around us, occupying the world in the same way that we do, entirely believable. It needs no frame around it for its reality to exist. Rather, it is the frame within which our realities play out.

The all-too real nature of architecture frames the role of the architect as a professional entity.

From the negotiations of permits and code to the production of construction information, to the managing of budgets, consultants and the construction process, the architect is assigned the pragmatic task of bringing a building into physical reality. Tracing the traditional professional role of the architect via, say, the job stages as outlined by a professional institution such as the RIBA, we see the articulation of the imaginary-to-real process of architecture. Beginning with Concept, and ending with Completion, an idea becomes a real part of the world. Following this standard professional procedure, architects take a concept or vision and manage the process though which scale, mass, material and space become part of the world around us.

But architecture itself manufactures reality in a more profound way. By expressing the economic, social and political ideologies of the society that creates it, and by organising these ideas into the spaces that we inhabit, architecture manufactures real worlds out of abstractions. To understand how architecture operates, fulfils this role as the interface between the imaginary forces that it embodies and the real form that it takes, we need to think of the way it performs, the way it enacts ideas into the world.

Enactment has two distinct definitions. First, it describes the theatrical acting out of a part or character, the dramatic representation of narrative through the performance of language, action and gesture. Secondly, it is the moment a law is passed into effect by a legislative body. We could understand architecture through these two definitions of enactment.

First, architecture performs through its representational, scenographic and symbolic qualities, which dramatise and communicate its narrative. Architecture's own languages are the gestures through which it acts out its role. Architecture's performance might be seen in the way it expresses itself—communicates its concerns through surface decoration, through massing and through its organisation. So, the Villa Savoye acts out the idea of the machine aesthetic by looking like industrial architecture, by performing a visual vocabulary as though it were a script and a costume. The rhetoric of the building is its fiction, the thing that is being acted; it gets all robed up, just like an actor, gesturing to its audience, speaking its lines. The villa also shows us how architecture acts to create a narrative arc, modulating the building's performance from scene to scene through the way it modulates movement through the spaces it creates. Architecture's organisation of signs and symbols in space generate readable meanings, dramatic effects and narrative, but its enactment does not happen on a stage. Architecture's act happens here in the same world that we live in. Its performance places the fictional (the imaginary, the idea) into the real space of the city. It *is* the real space of the city.

To enact is also to pass a law. It is the process of creating something that impacts on the possibilities or the prohibitions of the world within its jurisdiction. We know that in a practical sense architecture is subject to law. Building code, for example, sets out parameters that must legally be met. Permits and permissions direct and modify the construction process. Even the use of the term architect is controlled by law. But the argument here is not about the legal control of architecture; it's about the control that architecture exerts, its own legislative qualities, how architecture makes political will real in the world.

Intentionally or not, architecture is the physical manifestation of societal will, an enactment of the intentions of government, policy, capital, social convention and so on. It articulates this social, political and economic vision into the environmental frame within which society operates — the spaces in which we live. In the most direct sense, architecture permits and prevents the ways in which we use space. It defines what is acceptable and what is not. 'Love in the cathedral', as Bernard Tschumi once told us, 'differs from love in the street'. It differs because architecture makes the distinction between the two different types of space, setting out what is permitted or prohibited in either. Architecture organises space into discrete categories, distinct uses, particular forms of ownership. Its practical arrangement of programme into adjacencies and hierarchies at the scale of city and building arrange the ways in which we occupy these spaces. We sleep in bedrooms in arrangements of commonly agreed units, in spaces of a certain size, with particular relationships to our neighbours that are set out by architectural convention. In all of these ways, architecture both fulfils and enforces particular ways of occupying space. To quote Churchill again, 'we shape our buildings and our buildings shape us'. In highly specific ways buildings embed socio-political codes into space. A classroom spatially articulates the roles of teacher and pupil, defining the relationships between one and the other, both enabling and prescribing what each can or cannot do. It is in this sense that architecture acts as a form of law, governing behaviour within its jurisdiction. We are subject to architecture in the same way that we are subject to law.

B S Johnson's novel *Christie Malry's Own Double-Entry* lays out the base prohibition of architecture. The protagonist, Malry, is engaged in an exercise of tallying the debts that society owes him. He logs every perceived 'debit'—every hurt, injustice and unfairness—and against these notes his own form of 'credit', his personal revenge on the impositions that the world places on him. He makes one such entry after crossing Hammersmith Bridge and finding his desired route blocked by a building in his path. The debit is entered: 'May 1 — Restriction of Movement due to Edwardian Office Block — 0.05'. He explains the injustice of his situation: 'Who made me walk this way? Who decided I should not be walking seven feet farther that side, or three points west of nor-nor-east, to use the marine abbreviation? Anyone? No one? Someone must have decided. It was a conscious decision, as well. That is, they said (he said, she said), I will build here. But I think whoever it was did not also add, So Christie Malry shall not walk here, but shall walk there.' And he reclaims the debt accrued 'for standing this building in my way, too, limiting my freedom of movement, dictating to me where I may or may not walk in this street' with this credit: 'May 1 — Scratch on Facade of Edwardian Office Block: 0.05'. Malry's (hyper-paranoid) sensitivity demonstrates that every architectural decision is both a permission — in this case a programme and piece of urban fabric that allows certain things to happen — and a prohibition — the curtailing of any other possibilities of that site.

While buildings assume particular formulations, setting out within their boundary their permissions and their prohibitions, architecture as a discipline assumes an authority that is sovereign and uncontrollable, because it is impossible to escape. Architecture physically contains us whilst it, in the broad sense of the environment, cannot be contained. Architecture then assumes the role of the law-making process itself. It is the mechanism of enactment, the way legislation becomes law. Architecture manifests an imperative condition whose power is transcendent and absolute.

Both definitions of enactment, legal and theatrical, are simultaneously contained within architecture. Together, they suggest architecture's double role as performance and binding command. That is to say, cities, buildings and objects are simultaneously performances of an ideology and devices that manufacture particular ways of occupying space. Architecture, then, both represents and enforces the ideological conditions that it springs from. It embodies them in real space, exerting its power over territorial, temporal and personal dimensions. By making real the imaginary, the ideological and the fictional, it makes its artificial conventions appear to be a natural and necessary part of the world.

Architecture's fictions have 'real' consequences, and these consequences are the reality of the environments that it creates. In understanding architecture as a form of enactment, we can understand it as always active in manufacturing what we might describe as 'environmental ideology'—its actualising of social fiction. In understanding architecture as both performance and imperative, we understand it as an entity which *does*, rather than *is*.

More than a machine for living in, it is a machine that actualises and reproduces the realities it imagines. The fictions that architecture represents—whether Henry Ford's conception of American history, Le Corbusier's ideology of architecture as machine or the Johnson Wax conception of corporate organisation—are delivered into the real world though architecture's spatial and material organisation. Its narratives are performed through its gestures, its programmes script the possibilities of our occupation, setting out permissions and prohibitions so that we, like Christie Malry, become subject to its intentions.

THE THREE Rs: REPETITION, REPETITION, REPETITION

I have argued that architecture's own history is one of radical re-enactment of its own pasts—the Egyptian stone version of the wooden column, for example. But architecture's mode of repetition is not only confined to its past, nor to exceptional examples. We see it all around us. Perhaps the most ubiquitous and banal of contemporary architectural elements is the suspended ceiling. Patented by Donald Brown in 1961, it has since crept into almost every environment that requires heavy servicing. It provides a solution to a problem—what to do with the mess of services required to deliver reasonable levels of environmental comfort—that would otherwise need to be architecturally resolved. It hides and organises the wires, pipes and ducts and organises how these services interface with the occupiable space of a building through its positioning of sprinkler heads, smoke alarms, movement detectors, ventilation grills, light fittings and other accessories. The suspended ceiling is thus a practical device designed to cover space as cheaply and quickly as possible, without having to resolve any real architectural issues of how one material meets another.

The modular repetition of tiles of 600 x 600mm within an aluminium grid repeats to fill up the required space. Its repetition forms an apparent ceiling above our heads, its material quality giving it the appearance of being part of the built fabric even though it is, in fact, separate from the structure of the building. Unlike other decorative elements, the suspended ceiling is designed to look like a real ceiling. We could think of it in relation to the Egyptian column, as an image of architecture represented through a different material and technology—except that here the representation is not historically derived but is, rather, an image of an everyday contemporary ceiling. Along with its appearance, the suspended ceiling's ubiquity and its seamlessness within any given environment help to convince us of its ceilingness. In the way that it repeats an image of an actual ceiling, and in its modular repetition to form this image, it presents us with an example of how architecture uses repetition to become real. Unlike the Venturian image of architecture, where the billboard-facade (the sign) is expressed as a distinct element against the body of the building (the signified), here we see the sign and the signified, the image of the building and the building itself, coinciding as the same entity.

As architecture becomes part of the everyday landscape its quotidian banality asserts increasing degrees of reality. Non-stop re-enactment not only legitimises the conditions and ideologies that it embodies: it is a way of making real—of making architecture's innate syntheticness seem natural.

Architecture constantly repeats itself, re-enacts its own body in order to create itself. It repeats typologically, where genres of programme such as house or tower block are reiterated countless times. It repeats materially, where basic elements of construction such as brick or window frame recur both within a single building and across multiple sites. It repeats structurally, in column grids of A,B,A,B or A,BB,A,BB and so on. It repeats in the way that it constructs cities, street after street, in patterns that repeat whether in the most extreme form of the grid or in the grain of more ad hoc cities. Even in architecture's most novel formations, fundamental architectonic forms repeat: floor, wall, door and so on.

The <u>constant reiteration of architecture multiplies its sense of reality.</u> We might even say that architecture only achieves its reality through replication, when its forms, aesthetics or materialities appear in multiple sites, to the point where its qualities achieve total ubiquity — and architecture becomes a totalised environment on a planetary scale.

Repetition can be an intentional architectural tactic. Think of the modes of twinning that we can observe in the symmetry of plan or elevation in neo-classical architecture, where the building repeats as though a reflection of itself. Or think, perhaps, of Mies van der Rohe's Lake Shore Drive, where non-symmetrical repetition stands two identical versions of the same building at 90 degrees to one another. But the *ne plus ultra* architectural twin is the late Twin Towers — its self-similarity creates a condition where each building is an image of itself, both a replica and an original in equal measure. The doubling underlines architecture's presence. Through its doubling, it becomes more real.

Philip Johnson remarked 'modernism interested me because it was reproducible'. Like any system or language, like neo-classicism before it, modernism's reproducibility is part of its power. It produces an idea of universality, a totality of a logic played out in space and programme. If we imagine modernism's history as a set of ideas, of concepts, intentions that gradually become articulated into a clear architectural language, we can see the process of reiteration as the way in which it becomes real. And once it becomes 'real' its reality is impossible to escape. Modernism's repetition recalled its industrial origins — the repetition of Henry Ford's production line and the multiply reproduced object, the endless Model Ts that rolled off that line.

Certainly, Miesian architecture is characterised by its reproducibility, whether by Mies himself — as in the example of Lake Shore Drive, which gives us not only identical twin buildings at 860 LSD, but an almost-duplicate in 910, another pair of twins just around the corner, doubling an already doubled architecture — or by others applying Miesian principles.

Mies reproduced by Miesians can have a dislocating effect. In Chicago, the many Mies replicas by SOM, so accurate (and so plentiful), can disrupt one's sense of the city's geography, the same building apparently rearing up in multiple locations. Equally, we might remember, Philip Johnson's Glass House was a reproduction that pre-empted Mies's original: it realised the idea of the glass-walled house that Mies had invented in the Farnsworth House even before Mies's project had gone on site.

Not only do the buildings operate as replicas of each other, they are composed of self-similar components. In Mies, this sees columns, glass and concrete floor plates repeating endlessly up, down, left and right, only stopping at the limit of the building's envelope. When Mies said it was better to be good than original, perhaps he meant that originality is a problem because it impairs architecture's ability to provide a totalising system for the world, whereas repetition sharpens architecture's innately mimetic core. The effect of this endless repetition is to create a sensation of inevitability, of naturalising even the most radical of intentions. Perhaps what Mies meant by the word 'good' was 'real'.

Architecture's repetitive mode turns away from endless creativity, preferring instead the endless cycle of re-enactment that has the same quality as any ritual. Take the annual re-performance of the Trooping of the Colour, for example, where the monarch inspects the troops on the same day every year, with the same choreography. The symbolic performance of the pageantry of state and crown is multiplied because of its repetition: it gains its significance because it happens again and again. Likewise, the retelling of a joke transforms it into a ritual that has a social function beyond its humour. It makes it habitual, makes it part of our mental landscape, part of our own sensation of reality. The performance of a ritual writes it into the fabric of our everyday existence with an effect we could call mimetic hypnosis. It's real because it's everywhere, its endless repetition hypnotises us into seeing it as a natural truth.

Miesian repetition provides us with an extreme form of architecture's strategy of mimetic hypnosis. Yet we find the same condition pervades the entirety of the built environment. Modules of architecture from window to door, from wall to roof, from room to house, from house to street, from street to neighbourhood, from neighbourhood to city operate repetitively and mimetically. This repetitive mode is not explicitly one of re-enactment. That is to say, repetition is less explicit than re-enactment, in that it does not attempt to manufacture a copy or a replica of a past event or structure. In fact, there is no relationship of original to copy, of referent to reference, or even of signifier to signified—they are all equivalents, all enactments of each other.

Repetition is embedded brick upon brick, plank next to plank, sheet against sheet, in the fabrication of architecture's very body from pallets of modular construction industry products. Its scale and economies of construction mean it is built from self-similar elements that repeat in arrays. This rhythmic repetition across architecture's surface and through its body generates a hypnotic effect. Once may be exceptional, twice is coincidence, three or more and the serial nature of architecture begins to operate, each iteration reinforcing its fabrication of reality, its manufacture of the commonplace.

Architecture's repetitive and mimetic mode allows it to make an image of itself. As it repeats itself, architecture uses building as a medium to represent architecture. If at a grand historical scale we see this in the Roman replaying of the image of Greek architecture in new typologies, or in Renaissance architecture's re-performing of the image of classical architecture through its own contemporary scales and uses, we can see it also in the mundanity of contemporary construction. Here, it is architecture's own image, not its historical image, that is repeated: it is an enactment of itself rather than a re-enactment of something else. This self-referential repetition pictures the image of architecture as it becomes architecture. The sign and the signified coincide as the same thing, yet still operate as a semiological system. Being both itself and a sign of itself multiplies architecture's own argument for itself, makes it real in both symbolic and empirical senses at the same time.

Repetition traditionally serves to cement ideas. The repetition of a task allows us to practise and perfect it. It brings an easy fluidity, a sharpness and precision to the eventual performance, making it appear more natural. Yet we also know that repetition destroys original meaning. The tongue-twister, for example, by juxtaposing similar-sounding words and then demanding their speedy repetition, delivers a radical loss of fidelity to the original as the words collapse into noise. Repetition, then, does not necessarily condemn us to the production of direct simulations, but can be a method by which radical change is achieved.

In this way, repetition operates simultaneously to render the subject more natural and to drain it of its original meaning. Architecture's inherent repetitive quality hypnotises us into imagining that it is a landscape of inevitable and natural reality, rather than a fictional and ideological entity. Its constant re-enactment renders it unspectacular and mundane, making it appear inert. Its endless performance inoculates us against recognising the vast reserves of power, ideology and capital that architecture embodies.

NATURALISING
FICTION

Architecture is not about the world: it *is* the way in which the world is made. It is the mechanism by which our contemporary myths, the fictions that emerge from our political, social and economic circumstances, become physical. These social fictions are made real through architecture's enactment, through the way it performs and legislates. But in assuming such a profound sensation of reality, in becoming so inert, so naturalised, architecture obscures its mythic nature and psycho-cultural narrative. Architecture's sense of reality is so strong that it breaks any visible bond with the fictional. That is to say, when we look at a building, we are overwhelmed by its realness, utterly convinced by these figments of imagination.

A Great Roe could cross our path and we'd never know it, because the mythical beast seems indistinguishable from a common-or-garden biological lion. In the same way, architecture passes itself off as a natural entity, something that originates somewhere other than the myths that culture has written. Yet we should recognise that architecture is fundamentally <u>unnatural,</u> an utterly alien envi- ☞ ˙ ronment that is constructed conceptually just as it is constructed physically. It is an entirely synthetic invention with no intrinsic core other than one that we might invent. For all this, it assumes an effortless, entirely natural appearance. It feels, smells, looks and sounds like it is real. And in doing that it becomes real. We can think of its phenomenological performance as the way it makes itself real. As much as architecture performs as a technical environmental system and as a sensory thing, it also performs its social and ideological fictions. In performing them, it makes them real. Architecture's performative quality is the engine of its ability to manufacture the social fiction that we occupy, naturalising and legitimising it to the point where it becomes real.

Architecture, then, has no essence, contains no timeless truth. These too are simply myths that architecture has constructed in order to naturalise its unnaturalness. To believe architecture's fictions, to read them as natural and real, as fact rather than fictions that can be rewritten, is to misread architecture's full potential. Architecture as social fiction offers the ability to create realities that are far more powerful. It writes into reality the world that we wish to inhabit rather than the world we were born into. Architecture, just as Jay-Z says, speaks things into existence. The danger is that, without developing its own fictions, it simply services the narratives that bind us.

OTHER TITLES IN THE SERIES

THE ACTION IS THE FORM
VICTOR HUGO'S TED TALK
BY KELLER EASTERLING

ACROSS THE PLAZA
THE PUBLIC VOIDS OF THE
POST-SOVIET CITY
BY OWEN HATHERLEY

EDGE CITY
DRIVING THE PERIPHERY OF SÃO PAULO
BY JUSTIN MCGUIRK